THE CULTIVATION PERIOD
A SINGLE CHRISTIAN'S JOURNEY

By: Miracle Sims

Copyright © 2021 Miracle Sims. All rights reserved

No part of this publication may be reproduced, distributed, or transmitted in any form or by any means, including photocopying, recording, or other electronic or mechanical methods, without the prior written permission of the publisher, except in the case of brief quotations embodied in critical reviews and certain other noncommercial uses permitted by copyright law.

TABLE OF CONTENTS

PROLOGUE 1

THE BLACK WOMAN'S PRINCE CHARMING 4

PART 1 - PAST 5
- Chapter 1: Young but Not So Dumb 6
- Chapter 2: Making Mistakes on Purpose 12
- Chapter 3: The Man Who Got Me Back on Track 20
- Chapter 4: One Step Forward, Two Steps Back 24
- Chapter 5: Tripping Over My Own Two Feet 28
- Chapter 6: Rude Awakening 36

PART 2 - PRESENT 41
- Chapter 7: How Many Rehearsals Before the Show? 42
- Chapter 8: Enough Is Enough 49
- Chapter 9: Keeping A Spiritual Mind 55
- Chapter 10: Changes 60
- Chapter 11: Lesson Learned 69

PART 3 - FUTURE 74
- Chapter 12 Confirmation, And Blessings 75
- Chapter 13: Worth the Wait 80

EPILOGUE 85
SPECIAL THANKS 87
ABOUT THE AUTHOR 89

PROLOGUE

When I look back over my life, and I think things over, I realize that I have it pretty good, fantastic even. I am 23 with an apartment, job, career goals, no kids, no diseases, and... no man. For most of my life, I have been without a significant other. Not many boyfriends, but more than a few casual hookups or "situations", I call them. On one hand, I am embarrassed to think of the number, but for the record, I have only had sex once, which means that my "situations" only included foreplay, and when it comes to that, let us just say my lovers have spoiled me. I know it may be hard to believe that I have somehow gotten away with being pleased with little to no reciprocation, but hey, C'est la vie. Well, that is my life anyway. However, that is beside the point. The point is that at the end of the day, hookup situations are not what I want. I want marriage, I want love, and I want a relationship. On one hand, I may want all these things for the wrong reason... Sex, yeah, this little Christian woman thinks about sex... All the time... it is the main reason I end up in the "situations" to begin with. Even though I have been able to control myself to a certain extent thus far, it does not stop me from wanting it again later. Maybe I just want to feel connected to someone, or maybe I just have a problem. Either way, I am trying to control it even more than I ever have before. I am trying to wait to find that special man to fulfill my wildest fantasies, but it all seems to be just that. A fantasy, it seems that the pickings are slim, and the more I grow and learn every day the higher my standards are becoming. I wrote God a long list of what I want in a man. It may seem ridiculous, but I have learned you have to be specific when making a request to God. Seriously, plus I try to learn from those around me, so I have plenty of examples of dos and do nots and things I should and should not do. My last lover told me that I had/knew everything a man would want. The thing I have not figured out is if I am so great, then why am I single? On a spiritual note, it is not the time, and I have not met the right man. However, looking through natural eyes, it is all very confusing. Let's say the men in my past were being honest and that they do think I'm this great catch. Then why didn't they take things further with me? It doesn't make sense to let a good thing go, right? Then I could just turn it all around and blame them by saying that they told me these kind words as an attempt to get into my panties. However, I've been a willing participant when it comes to being pleased, and even though there's been plenty of times I've left men hanging by just saying no, I'm a little woman, so they could've easily taken advantage' Which I thank, and praise God that scenario hasn't happened. I know that my last two "situations" were great men, but they did not want a relationship. I guess I just keep attracting the wrong "good men", and unfortunately nowadays, the Christian men I have met would rather be my mentor or big brothers. There was an older man I was interested in, but he is still stuck on his ex and isn't looking to start anything new with me, and the younger guy just wants to have fun… C'est la vie. This book is the story of my past, present, and goals for my future, and things I have learned along the way on my journey to live successfully single.

THE BLACK WOMAN'S PRINCE CHARMING

BY MIRACLE SIMS

How come when it comes to love and fairy tales to the black woman it seems to be just that...a dream? Make-believe. Thoughts so far-fetched, things too impossible to be true.

Where's the black Woman's prince charming? Is that dream too good to be true? Is it in vain to look for a man who is loving, respectful, and understanding of his woman's wants and needs?

Is there a man out there for her that can appeal to her spiritually, emotionally, and physically? Is she expecting too much if she wants this fairy tale man? Have all her prospects become so focused on sex and/or each other to be the king that she so desperately wants, and needs, for him to be?

Does she have to lower her standards and the value of herself to find what most women hold on to as love, but is a weak substitute involving only the physical aspect of what she hopes to become a lasting relationship?

There must be someone out there for her because she knows that all men aren't the same...well, she has faith and hopes that all men aren't the same.

However, if there isn't any proof of this around her then is she waiting in that tall, lonely tower in vain? Will she ever be awakened from her everlasting sleep?

PART - I
PAST

CHAPTER - 1
YOUNG BUT NOT SO DUMB

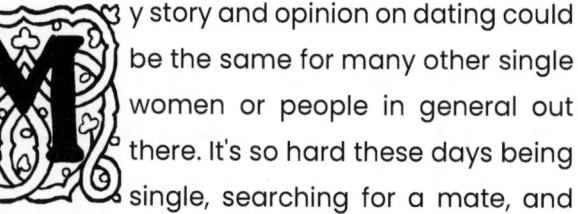

y story and opinion on dating could be the same for many other single women or people in general out there. It's so hard these days being single, searching for a mate, and looking for love in all the wrong places. My poem "The Black Woman's Prince Charming" expressed a lot of my issues, and questions about dating, and men. However, I also had a lot of questions for myself. The main one is: How did I end up in this position of randomly hooking up with random guys? As I mentioned in the prologue "situations" are not what I want in the long run, and they have not led to the type of relationship that I want. To figure the answer out I concluded that to understand why I feel the way I do, and how I have grown to be the woman I am today, I must start at the beginning

I grew up in a small town where people joke that it seems like there is nothing much to do, but go to school, and have sex. I am grateful to have a God-fearing mother who cared enough to teach me right from wrong. She kept such a hold on me that I knew in advance that I could not do the things that everyone else did. I cannot say that I had the perfect childhood, but I can say that I was able to avoid many of the things that most children could get into at an early age. Aside from occasional babysitters, and family members, most of my time was spent with my mother, and my sister.

When I go back mentally to look at the root of where my problem with sexual situations possibly stemmed from. I found that it is most likely from the rare moments when I was not under my mother's wing. Though those times were few, that was the beginning of my struggle. It was in those times that a seed was planted, and I experienced what I now know as being molested.

I am thankful that my story does not include a man taking my virginity by rape, but the fact that my molester was a woman does not change the fact that my innocence was taken all the same. From what I remember I wasn't forced, as in held down and taken advantage of, but I was touched and kissed in ways that I shouldn't have been as a child. Confessing this truth may not have anything directly to do with why I am single. However, I believe it plays a major part in my mindset and some of the future decisions I made. For a long time, I never talked about what happened, and even now it seems like it may have all been a dream. In the process of writing, I debated about asking, and talking to the woman that was involved. However, I feel that the point is that I have defined my problem, and where it came from, and I feel like all I need at this point are solutions. My first piece of advice is, "Do not dwell on the past, learn from the situation, and move forward."

I've witnessed many examples of teenage pregnancies, and girls that have been taken advantage of that encouraged me to hold on to my virginity throughout high school, and the bulk of my adult life. I knew that there were too many consequences to having sex that I was not ready to deal with. My friends would share their experiences, and that was enough for me until I had my own. I experienced what most would call going to first base in the 10th grade. Things did not go too far at all given the place it happened, school. The bible says in 1 Corinthians 7:1 "... it is good for a man not to touch a woman..." Now I can fully see exactly why that is. For me, that touch has been addictive. I crave that touch, and the feeling I get when I am being touched. My fantasies had become reality and it helped me to understand how the other girls may have ended up in positions that they could not or did not want to get out of. All the stories from my friends, and the reality of having a guy touch me intimately, whether I touched him back or not, was the beginning of my "situations". To look at this all on a spiritual level, I was feeding my flesh with the sexual escapades of my friends, the sex books that passed around like wildfire throughout my school days, and creating poems about my "situations", and my fantasies. After the first base situation, one situation after another began to happen over the rest of my years in high school. It led to several things I'm ashamed to be associated with like kissing another girls' boyfriend and being caught in school with a guy with his pants down, literally. However, since I was "single" I did not think much of it. I did not have many boyfriends in school, and the ones I had I did not feel connected or committed to, and unfortunately, I entered college with the same mindset.

I know I can't change you, and you must find your own way.

Maybe you'll join me on this path another day.

But know that my whole reason for letting you go is because

I love you...

Excerpt from: The Last Attempt (My Goodbye)
By: Miracle Sims

CHAPTER - 2
MAKING MISTAKES ON PURPOSE

I rarely had the opportunity to act on any of the feelings I was having with anyone besides myself via masturbation because I was always with my mother. Wherever she went my sister, and I went, and it was mostly to church. That is a blessing because only God knows where I would be if it were not for my mothers' teachings. My mother is an Evangelist, and most people are familiar with the ongoing rumor about preachers' kids leaving home, running wild, and being rebellious. I cannot say that I had in my mind to do those things; however, in God's eyes, I am sure he saw it that way. When I left home for college, I felt invincible. I say that because I had the mindset that certain things couldn't happen to me. I'm sure we've all felt that way about one thing or another. At the time I felt that if I wasn't having sex, I wasn't doing anything wrong. So, I continued to fool around all the while "maintaining my virginity", but I realize now that it all is wrong, according to the bible even letting my mind go there is wrong.

Along with learning that being touched sexually felt good at an early age, the molestation also led to my attraction to women. At one point, during my school years, I finally decided to verbalize what happened in my childhood, and the feelings I was having. Back then, my mother started a non-profit organization, she would gather the youth, and talk to them about their issues, and spiritually encourage them. At that time, she had a couple of women helping her, and while we were on a field trip with the group, I ended up connecting with one of the mentors. We talked about so much during that trip, and I felt so comfortable that I decided to talk to her about the feelings I was having. This was a huge deal to me because at that time I never even wrote about them in my diary. However, she took the conversation, and subject with ease, and was very encouraging. She let me know that she went through the same situation when she was younger. However, the blessing that our conversation was to me turned sour quickly, because my mother felt disrespected because, I talked to someone else, and unfortunately, at that time, I did not feel comfortable telling her. Out of respect to me, the woman would not speak about it either. However, Eventually, I broke down, and told my mother, but when I did. All she did was pray for me, and we never really talked about it again. As far as I know, my mother has never experienced anything like my situation, and that is one of the main reasons I did not talk to her in the beginning.

So of course, after that incident, and not fully understanding or considering the consequences that would come from acting on the feelings I was having I ended up engaging in a homosexual relationship. At the time I only saw it as another "situation" the same as I did with men. It felt good to talk to my female lover; we were raised the same way when it came to having Christian mothers. We connected first as friends and became so close to the point where we would sleep in the same bed. The reason that started was innocent enough, we were usually up so late talking that it would only make sense for her to sleepover in my room. However, when we became roommates, we ended up doing the same thing. One night we were talking and on the verge of sleep, but I could not fall asleep mainly because she was breathing on my neck. It could have been on purpose, or she could have just been sleeping, either way, I was turned on. I was turned on to the point that I kissed her. After this first kiss. She asked me why I did that, and I was embarrassed, because other than the way I felt, I didn't know. Nevertheless, that began us experimenting with each other, and eventually, it started to feel like a relationship. We never said that it was, but we did express that the feeling was mutual. Our time together felt good, but it didn't feel right. Some may say it was my conscience, but I feel it was the Spirit dealing with me. No matter what situations I would get myself into I could never feel fully comfortable, because of the twinge of doubt, and guilt, and the voice within that tells me, what I am doing is wrong. We would talk about it a lot, but she never seemed to care as much as I did, despite being raised the same way I was... There were a few reasons I ultimately turned around and ended our physical relationship. Reason 1 is that in my fantasies I never pictured a relationship forming from my lesbian experience and that is exactly what we felt like, and at one point, it felt so right. That I questioned everything I had been taught throughout my life. Therefore, because of my inner conflict, I decided to seek God for clarity, and answers concerning these feelings. I wanted to find out for myself what the Bible said concerning homosexuality. That's another side note. If you're confused about something, seek God. It's ok to have questions because questions are the start of development. I have yet to read the whole bible, but I'm a witness that Matthew 7:7 ..." seek, and ye shall find..." rings true. I started to read the bible looking for some form of clarity, and verses practically jumped out at me clearly stating Gods' opinion on the matter. There was no way that I could not deny that the path I was on was wrong, it hurt, but I let that part of our friendship go. I hoped that she would do the same, but to this day, she is still dating women as far as I know. For a long time, I felt guilty and responsible for that. However, I have grown to realize that we all make our own decisions.

Another reason I gave up what we had is that I am very much attracted to men. To be honest, I never stopped having situations with them while things were going on with her because of course, I was "single ". So those two reasons alone were enough for me to get off that path. However, it was not enough for me to stop seeking out pleasure and allowing whoever was willing to give it to me.

The first time I gave a little reciprocation to the point where he climaxed was after college, and it was with my little hands. Hand jobs are apparently what grade school kids do these days, and I do not know who I should feel sadder for, for them, or me? Nevertheless, I never had any complaints at that point, and I saw him "finish" so apparently, I did something right. In those days, I would become bold enough to get naked, and take showers with him and I guess he was strong enough to handle not having more of me than I was willing to give, my hands. I find it hilarious that I haven't mentioned anything about our conversations! He was the first guy I felt could be "the one". He was tall, dark, and handsome. The first time we went on a date, he suggested that we go to the lake, and it was there that we sat on a hammock, and talked for hours, and I thought that was unique, and that he was charming. I am not sure exactly what he felt about me, but I felt so connected to him that even after he left the state, I mentally waited for his return. However, he never established that we were in a relationship, so I still had "situations" going on even though I thought about him. It was then when I met a man that helped me turn around my whole life.

"When you start giving up everything that's keeping you from being who you're supposed to be...you will start living, and not just be breathing to death"

-Anonymous

CHAPTER - 3

THE MAN WHO GOT ME BACK ON TRACK

When it comes to this man, Frank, I will call him, it is a touchy subject because my mind is still weak for him at times. He's the second man that I felt could be my one, even more than the first because I've connected with him spiritually which was the first time, I've discussed Christ with a lover. I met him in church. We had this sudden connection during the service, and he approached me afterward, and we exchanged numbers, and we ended up spending time together soon after. I flirted with him as usual, but that is where things took a different turn.

There were times that we made out, and I wanted him to touch me like any other man in this situation usually would. However, instead, he would minister to me about how I did not belong to him, and how it was not right for him to touch me in that way because he was not my husband. I did not understand how he could say he was not my husband when it felt like he could be. However, every time we would end up in situations he would minister to me, and do what I had done to men when it came to having sex. Deny me. The more he denied, and respected me the more I wanted him physically until one night he gave in, and touched me, pleased me, gave me what I wanted.

Soon after he suggested that we should not continue to be friends because I was affecting his walk with Christ. I had never been cut off because of my actions. Fooling around, and foreplay was what I was used to with men. It was what they wanted, and I assumed it was what he wanted too. That is when I had to tell myself the things that everything, I was doing was wrong. Because of my actions, I was pushing a good man that could have been more than a friend away. From then on, I decided to work on myself. He saw that I had made a change, and we are still good friends to this day. I consider him a mentor, and for the most part, I have gotten over feeling as if he is my one. However, that still did not stop me from completely ending my "situations". It seems I took that one step forward just to take two steps back.

"It's not good to seek the feeling of love. Especially when you don't fully understand love. Sex and fleshly sins are not needs they are wants, and wants are not always important..."

-Miracle Sims

CHAPTER - 4

ONE STEP FORWARD, TWO STEPS BACK

In my next relationship, I ended up taking risks and doing things I had never done before. All mainly, because he held the title "boyfriend" It had been years since anyone had that place in my life. Sometimes when we are in a relationship, we feel obligated to do certain things, because the world is doing it. However, just because something is common does not make it right. Granted, before him, the last time I had a "boyfriend" was in high school, and that person lived in a different city. This was the first time I was able to be around my "boyfriend" all the time, and anytime.

He was a decent person, was very cute, nice body, and had a nice smile. It was around my birthday that I met him, so I invited him to my celebration. This was soon after my promise I made to myself to start doing things the right way, but when he attended my party, and we danced I was back into my old self and decided to take advantage of that situation having it in my mind that it would be like a birthday gift. However, to my surprise, a relationship formed after. I think we both had been single for so long that we clung to each other for that affection and attention we had both been missing. However, because I had failed at starting things the right way with him, I could not fully embrace our relationship, not without letting him know what I was supposed to be doing, so I ended up writing him a letter explaining all the things I had been working on before I met him. That is when things started to become awkward between us, I thought that it was because he felt responsible for my failure. So, I spent the rest of the relationship trying to prove that he was not my problem and that he was not at fault, but by doing that, I continued to do the things I wanted to change.

As I look at all the things in my life, everything I did and went through happened like a domino effect. Each step ultimately led to the other, and eventually, I had passed the point of no return, my virginity. 7 months into a relationship that I knew started wrong I gave myself to this man and no offense to him, but it was not worth it. Not to say the experience was bad. However, I do not remember feeling satisfied or fulfilled after. I thought the whole point of sex was to feel some sort of overwhelming sense of gratification at the end. 22 years of waiting, and I gave myself away to this man, and to add insult to injury we broke up a week later. I am ok, but the main thing that disappoints me about the whole situation is that I know in the back of my mind that if I had exercised the strength to say no that one time, I would probably still be a virgin right now. One thing always leads to another, because going all the way with him made me too comfortable with the next man.

I giggle and smirk after realizing that I'm feeling you, with all five senses...

Excerpt From: Five Senses
Written By: Miracle Sims

CHAPTER - 5
TRIPPING OVER MY OWN TWO FEET

The next man in my life that I felt could be "the one" appealed to me in just about every way. I think all the things I liked about him blinded me to the things that were not necessarily right for me. He seemed so out of my range that when my fantasies about him became reality I did not want to let go. I felt like I was having a high school crush. Things started decently with him; I did not let my first date with him be his house. I let him know when I did come to his house that I did not want to meet him too late, and I let him know upfront my views, and what I was looking for. However, we ended up in some of the same situations I always did, only this time I was making mistakes that were even more serious.

I loved spending time with him, with and without the physical interactions. I am glad that we talked and got to know each other. After those first few decent interactions of "playing it safe" and keeping up my guard we could not seem to keep our hands off each other. Because of that, he limited the times we saw each other. He said that his "attraction to me was a distraction". However, most of the time that is exactly what I felt that he was to me, a distraction, and temptation, but that didn't stop me from wanting to be around him and wanting to get to know him. In the back of my mind, I told myself that getting to know him was all that I wanted.

However, both of our bodies were saying something completely different. He was a lot stronger than I was mentally I must admit. I think he made up his mind about me from the beginning. I say this because though we got close to many things. He held his ground and withheld from me one main interaction. Kissing... I found that interesting, all I could think about when he would kiss me everywhere, but my lips was the scene in the movie "Pretty Woman" when Vivian wouldn't kiss Edward, she said she didn't do it because it was "too personal" I don't know if this was just something he did with me or what, but I couldn't help but remind myself of how interesting it was that this man wouldn't let his guard down to kiss my lips. However, I let my guard down to the point where he almost penetrated me without a condom. We came so close to sex twice, and both times, he ended up being the bigger person by stopping the situation. The last time I saw him he left my place so quickly acting as if he would not be able to contain himself if he touched me again, even to hug me goodbye. Therefore, he did not. Seconds after he left, he called me and told me how he did not want to start anything new, because he still had feelings for his ex. Understandable, because that is something we discussed in the beginning. However, to hear that right after he almost penetrated me without a condom was enough to snap me out of my fantasy world.

Sometimes I find it overall better to write whatever I am feeling, because it helps me to evaluate what I want to say, and how I want to say it. Therefore, after his phone call, I wrote him a goodbye text. I let him know that I was glad that we had gotten to know each other, but I did not like or want to be a distraction. I told him that I was done with my part of the mind games that we were playing, and that I would be ok if I did not hear from him. Sure enough, to this day, I have not heard from him that I know of. I did get an anonymous message that seemed to be his style, but as far as direct contact, there has been none. I did not send the message trying to get the last word. It was more for the whole situation to have some form of closure in my mind. He seems to have moved on, but despite my attempt at closure, the process of keeping him out of my mind has been difficult.

There are a few reasons that I have not been able to keep this man off my mind despite our last encounter. Reason one was that I was still attracted to him. When I think about it, I think I was attracted to the idea of him. But aside from being attracted, the main reason this man stayed on my mind after the no condom situation is that I was nervous about whether I slipped up to the point where my life would be off track. The ultimate roadblock for everything that I have been working on in my life would be to be pregnant. As much as I love kids and babies, I am not ready to be a mother. I am not saying that if I were in that situation, I would not take care of my child, and strive to be a good mother. However, my current situation cannot have a child mixed in, I debated about getting a pet once and concluded that I am "too busy" so I can't imagine what having a child would be like right now. Months after the incident I was nervous about the possibility of being pregnant or if something worse had happened from our encounter. My monthly visitor took its time coming, and my mind was playing all kinds of tricks on me in the process of waiting for it to come. Every slight imperfection with my body became a sign of me being pregnant. I know that being pregnant shouldn't be seen as a curse, but if I wanted to take the route of possibly ending up a single mother I could've done it at home in my hometown, and not miles away, and in the place in my life where I have so many goals, dreams, and things I would like to do. I know that God kept me throughout that situation; because anything could have happened as I straddled that man, both of us naked, neither one of us saying anything about a condom. No, we technically did not go all the way, but he could have grabbed me, taken me at that moment, and subjected me to whatever diseases he may or may not have. I do not know, because we never talked about anything like that. We both could have given in to the temptation to go all the way, and I could have been pregnant right now. I could have gotten pregnant from being that close to him. That may be extreme, but you never know. All of this was on my mind during the months after our encounter, and he is off doing his own thing and most likely not thinking about me.

When my monthly visitor finally arrived, the day after it ended, I woke up the next morning vomiting. I think it ended up being food poisoning, but that did not help my thoughts. Finally, I let the idea of being pregnant go after the crimson tide came twice after the incident. This man still finds his way into my mind from time to time, and I am not exactly happy that we do not have any contact anymore. However, I know that overall, this is the best situation for me.

I have no idea what my family, that man, or I would have done if I were pregnant. I can imagine several scenarios, the ideal scenario if I were pregnant would be for him to decide to make me his wife, but do you know which scenario I prefer? The one I am in now. Sure, I still think about him; However, I know that God through him did the best thing for me by letting me go and leaving the way he did. Even calling me right after confessing about the feelings he has for his ex was a great thing to do for me, because all those actions put things in perspective for me. It opened my eyes to the road I was on, and the path that I was headed. The fact of the matter is I can continue to go down the road of meaningless hookups that will eventually lead to destruction, or just wait on God to fulfill his plan, and promise. Just because I have been blessed to not have any major or "bad things" happen from the situations I have been in thus far it does not mean that it will always be that way, and if anything, "bad" does happen I know that it will not be because "God is taking his protection away", or "turning his back on me". It will be because I continued to place myself into situations, and temptations that lead to sin that will ultimately lead to death. Which are the words of God and not my words therefore it is just foreshadowing the inevitable.

Ask, and it shall be given you; seek, and ye shall find; knock, and it shall be opened unto you: For every one that asketh receiveth; and he that seeketh findeth, and to him that knocketh it shall be opened.

Matthew 7:7-8
King James Version (KJV)

CHAPTER - 6
RUDE AWAKENING

One morning during the process of writing notes for this book. I was thinking of all the things I did not like about being single, and all the things men have told me over the years that I did not understand. I took a break from writing to check my messages because I decided to make notes about a few of the messages I have gotten online from men again that I did not fully understand. While I was checking up on those things, I decided to check my daily message called "God wants you to know..." Which are daily inspirational quotes, and messages. It is so amazing that sometimes, those things hit the nail on the head. The message I received that morning stated something along these lines "It's great that you pray to God, now stop talking, so you can hear Him talk to you." It kind of shook me, because it was so blunt, and to the point. At that time my prayers and thoughts did consist of constant questions for him. I felt God telling me once that I didn't ask the men I fooled around with half as many questions as I asked him. Maybe deep inside I did not want to know whatever truth they had to share. I tried to justify my questioning Him, by saying that I question Him because He is the one that is supposed to have all the answers. However, that morning, I could allow no excuse to come into my head. So, I looked up, and said OK God, what do

you want me to know? He sent me a vision so plain, and so surreal that it changed the whole dynamic and motive of this book. I saw myself giving myself sexually to someone who did not care about me. After we had sex, he pushed me away. I saw myself in tears, continued loneliness, and then murdered. Which I interpreted to mean a life cut short somehow. That vision is not how I want my life to end up or be. I know that God's plan is better than any I can ever dream of or try to make happen. Yes, my story gives me experience, but I should have learned from all the stories of the surrounding people without having to experience them for myself. I have an idea of what I am supposed to do instead of the things I was doing, and I am currently living to change my life, and re-write my future to make it a story of triumph, victory, and success.

I plan to spend my time wisely, and not continuously place myself into situations that never lead to anything good. Instead of focusing, so much on being single like it is a negative thing I can and will embrace it. I have married friends that tell me all the time that they wish they were in my situation, so they could take more time for themselves. That is exactly what single women or single people, in general, should do. Take the time for God, and yourself, get closer to him and focus on the things you want to do with your life. Do whatever it is that you want to do! I realize that God is the best planner, and if you make

His will your will and his wants your wants, He will ultimately give you what you want! He will give you the desires of your heart. I know firsthand that it's hard being single especially when you don't want to be, but obviously, I'm supposed to be doing something else besides worrying about getting a man, and so are you. Instead of feeling sorry for yourself and continuing to drown yourself in whatever sin, you are in. Take charge of your life! Free yourself from that bondage! Sin is bondage, not obeying God. Sin comes from yielding to our desires, and temptations. The choice is yours, life or death. I'm choosing life, and I'm getting better at keeping myself out of my old situations, making better decisions, and getting rid of bad habits. You cannot expect different results by doing the same things.

...NO! I'm good, but I bet you wish that I would have a one-night affair, but I won't go there...

Lyrics from: Miracle Sims- "I'm Good"

PART - II
PRESENT

CHAPTER - 7
HOW MANY REHEARSALS BEFORE THE SHOW?

One thing I have learned in my life is that things will come in our path to distract and tempt us when things are going well. You would not believe all the attempts, and things I have gone through since I have cracked down on sticking to my decision to live and do things the right way. One Sunday evening I was feeling joyful. I had a great morning, I went to church, heard a great message, and even got a free lunch! Therefore, I say again I was feeling good! I went to surprise a friend at his job to tell him a happy birthday, and afterward, as I was walking to my car an older man caught my eye. I said hello, and proceeded to keep walking, but he stopped to make conversation. I listened, but the whole thing felt awkward. He said he wanted to hang out and he asked if I could wait until he was done in the store, I said OK before I realized it, I know that I could have left, and I probably should have, but I did not want to be rude, so I decided to just wait until he came back to tell him I was going to head home. He came back, and just when I was going to tell him the above, he asked me if I wanted to "fool around", I was shocked, I couldn't believe he asked me this in broad daylight in a Walgreens parking lot with me in a huge winter coat! I told him I do not do things like that and dismissed him. However, my first thought was what is it about me that made him approach me like that? I was about to let it get to me, and start to feel sad, and angry. However, I decided to turn it around, because I did not want to let that interaction ruin my day and steal my joy. Sometimes the devil is so predictable I feel like the things that I am doing have to be bigger than I know because he is constantly bothering me.

With all the negative things that happen in the world these days, we as humans get the impression that the devil is powerful. It is hard to wait on Gods' will; it seems I am tempted every day. It's bad enough that I must deal with the things that come into my head, but he sends more temptations through other people to feed that issue, such as, tempting me with the past and present men that seem to be coming out of the woodworks. For the most part, I have nipped the men in my life in the bud. I have explained, and have been standing on mine, and Gods' word well.

There are times when I get texts and pictures from old flings, but I am not into mind games. I have always felt that dating was to find someone to marry. I do not see the point of dating someone you cannot see yourself with in the future. There was a comedian I was performing with in this play recently, and we had this little side joke/flirt session going. We would tease each other about having a "private rehearsal" to practice a kissing scene (that we did not have). One day the subject came up while we were chatting online, but this time he was very bold with his advances, he asked, "When were we going to rehearse lovemaking?" To go along with the rehearsal, and "show" theme. I responded saying," Let me check with the director." Then I said, "The Director (God) doesn't approve of fornication." He quickly responded making a comment explaining that he meant just foreplay, not penetration. Then I asked him and myself a brilliant question. "How many rehearsals do I have to have before the show?" I heard that this man is already dating someone, so there is no way that he could be serious about me. So how many times do I have to waste my time with men that do not care? How many times will I keep allowing the temptations to control me? Sometimes I feel like I am over practicing, and that I am ready for the show of a real relationship, and marriage.

I believe that if I could be married right now, I would be. I want to be, there is a part of me that is just so ready to have that type of relationship. Everywhere I go I see couples loving each other. With every click of a mouse, online links to dating sites pop up. On TV, there are a plethora of shows about weddings these days. Often as I lie alone either on my couch or bed, I try to imagine what my husband will be like. He never really has a particular look, but I imagine the things he says to me, and how he makes me feel. I think of how he touches and looks at me. Thinking about these things usually makes me feel one of two ways. Either frustrated or aroused. The reason I sometimes get frustrated with my thoughts of the future is because the visions sometimes seem so unreal. As if the visions I play in my mind could never be reality. I believe that it could happen, but the "too good to be true" doubt always seems to come in. I saw an old fling recently, and in came the feelings of loneliness, and self-doubt. The last time I thought about him, I checked out his profile online and saw that he is currently in a relationship. He also had pictures of his significant other displayed, which tells me that he is committed. He shook my hand that day like we were meeting for the first time, but I honestly, did not need any more than that handshake anyway. I kept the interaction short and semi-sweet for my sanity. He tried to make conversation. I guess it was also his way of checking me out, but that does not matter, because he is taken so there is no point in entertaining the thought of him. I started to question God again about me, and this whole relationship thing. Do I want what I cannot have? Am I asking for too much? What is it about me that is keeping me from going to that next level? Is it my looks? What am I supposed to do when I feel like this?

Aside from the doubt that constantly comes, it seems that I am always on the hunt. Searching for "the one" wondering if every man I meet "him" If I have the least bit of attraction to a man, he is a prospect until proven not. I want to stop looking for love. I want to just let it happen when it's supposed to happen. I want to just love God, and myself enough, because I know I can't control how anyone feels it's either there or it's not. It feels like I keep building myself up to be let down.

"If it is to be, it's up to me"

-Coach Obie Johnson

CHAPTER - 8
ENOUGH IS ENOUGH

When I become aroused by my thoughts it would usually lead to some form of masturbation either physically or mentally. I tend to think a lot, as I am sure you can tell, and in these times of temptation, my thought process usually goes like this. It starts with just wanting to feel good. I tend to imagine the things I want, my future, and my husband as I mentioned before, because if only for a moment it gets my mind off my life, and whatever I'm going through at the time. The thoughts make me feel good. Seems innocent enough, right? Well then comes all the random freaky thoughts, images I have seen, things I heard, even things I have done. That gets my body and mind in the mood, and in the mindset.

It is hard to deal with the fact that I am the problem. It is so easy to give in to temptation. It is easier to just touch yourself than to get up. However, just because it is easier does not make it right. I have realized that failing in the small things, keeps me stagnant and away from the big things. I did not use to feel bad after I masturbated, because once again I assumed it was better than having sex. However, sin is sin, and wrong is wrong. God is not going to bless a mess, and I was messed up. My mindset was wrong, and my life was headed nowhere. I had to decide for myself that enough was enough and that since

I now know plainly where I have been falling short. I had to make a change for the better.

Now that I have taken that long look in the mirror, I have been focused on using every day to learn and grow. It is an everyday process, but despite the constant temptations that have been thrown my way, I have been standing strong, and confident. And every day has been a blessing, because of it. Yes, the spiritual attacks will continue to come, they will come more because you've decided to change. The enemy does not like or want us to give our lives to God and do God's will. Nothing is stopping you from changing your life, but you. The only way to get out of your rut, and to stop doing the things that are not pleasing in God's sight is to DO IT!

It is so amazing to see God at work in my life. I have learned so much since I have decided to make these life changes. On the day I was tempted and tested, but I did not fail. I realized that overall, not failing felt so much better than the feeling I would have felt if I had given in. Oh, do not get me wrong, the process hurt! I questioned myself, God, my faith. I even ended up crying. In case you are wondering I am talking about the masturbation problem. Truthfully, it was one of the main things that I have had to deal with because it does not help my walk with Christ. Someone out there may deal with things that may seem to be worse habits than my masturbating. However, God sees it all to be the same...murder and lying is all on the same level to Him. So whatever habit that you need to break I just want to encourage, and let you know that you can do it with God's help.

I know that if I continued to dwell on the inner dialogue I would have been back in my old routine. Thinking of the past and dreaming of the future just enough to get off. However, for one more day I did without that habit, and I got a lot done that day. I ended up doing chores and I even worked on a creative project. Which were both things I had been putting to the side.

My thought process has changed since I have started to recognize the traps that come my way. Now when I start to have the thoughts that tempt me into old habits do you know what comes to mind? Quotes of encouragement things like; "be patient", "be faithful in the small things", etc.... Now I have thoughts that ultimately kill whatever mood that may start to arise within me. It is for the best I know, but I must admit other thoughts try to enter my mind to counter the encouragement such as "Why do I care? It seems like no one else does." "Everyone else can have moments of pleasure, why can't I?" There is no doubt in my mind where those thoughts come from. Nevertheless, once you know the truth it is hard to comfortably go back to lies. So, despite the sense of disappointment that sometimes arises after denying myself, knowing that I beat the temptation is great! My brain controls my body, not the other way around!

I keep referring to sexual problems, and situations, because that has been my #1 struggle with being single. All these things kept my focus from where it should have been. God and his plan for me and my life are where my focus should be. What is the thing that you are dealing with? I do not know, and I cannot change your mind for you. I just pray that you lay aside whatever it is that is weighing you down. Choose life, I did, and I have never felt freer. Temptations come, and go, they will always be there, but the beauty of it all is that we do not have to yield to the temptations. We can have victory over them. I want victory! Don't you? I mainly want to make sure I am doing what I am supposed to/need to do in this life, and I feel that I am on the right track. Overcoming my daily temptations inspires me to keep going.

"You have a dog made of flesh inside of you and a dog made of spirit fighting each other constantly Do you know which one is going to win? The one you are feeding. If you feed your flesh, it will be stronger than your spirit, and if you feed your spirit, it will defeat your flesh."

– Anonymous

CHAPTER - 9
KEEPING A SPIRITUAL MIND

I heard a news report not too long ago about a robber coming into a Christian bookstore demanding money. The owner of the shop commanded the devil to leave. I believe that her words were "In the name of Jesus I command you to get out of my shop! Do you know what that robber did? He fled. It shouldn't be as much of a surprise as it is. There are many accounts in the bible about this behavior from the devil and his spirits. Again, I say that with all the negative things that go on in the world we as humans get the impression that the devil is powerful. The truth is that he can do no more than we allow him to do! We can stand as boldly as that shop owner, and rebuke Satan because we already have the victory! There may be some cases that it may be hard to rebuke the devil boldly, such as rape situations, and human trafficking. However, I believe God can and will take care of his own, in all situations. I've never experienced those things, and I pray I never will. I can imagine both of those situations and others, that would be terrible, and the last thing that someone would want to do is be told to trust God. But God is a keeper, and a healer I know He will lead, and guide you to your purpose. I can only talk about my experiences, and the lessons I've learned. However, if you are a survivor of those things, I want you to know that you are not alone. Your testimony can very well help and save someone else.

It's hard to think of things spiritually, but the truth is there is a spiritual base to everything in this life. One day I decided to break it all down so here's what I've learned and realized about my situation that ultimately helped me decide to get on the right track. There are only two kinds of people on earth: those who love God, and those who don't. This is basically how He sees it, and the devil's whole purpose is to steal, kill, and destroy. So, when it comes to me and the life, I was living day after day which included thinking about men, masturbating, and beating myself up mentally. Those things were all devices to keep me and my mind from where they should've been, which is on God. So, every day I've been making strides. I'm focusing on having, and keeping a spiritual mind, mainly because when one's mind is on the spirit it's easier not to be tricked by the thoughts and things of this world. For instance, the other night I got a late-night text from an old fling. I heard the message come in, and before I read it, I knew who it was, but I didn't even pick up the phone until I was mentally prepared to deal with whatever this man had to say. When I was ready, I read the message and responded. The opportunity to text sexual things was there, but I didn't take it, and those small steps helped to turn the whole situation around and I ended up witnessing to him! Once our conversation was on a spiritual level, I told him "There is so much going on, on a deeper level that most people don't care about or understand that is so important. I told him that even our conversation was an example because if my mind or his allowed the spirit of lust to come in, the whole dialogue between us would've been different, and ultimately another trap." I believe that this is true with every situation. The more I learn, the more I feel at peace, and grow to love who I am now!

"Figuring out your purpose? He (God) is your purpose...!... I'm living for my savior. I've found nothing else worth living for...I loved God, but my life said I hated Him."

-Jasmine Jackson

CHAPTER - 10
CHANGES

I've been working on keeping my huntress skills in check. My "situations" still come to my mind, but I try my best not to dwell on those thoughts. One day I was eating lunch alone at work, and there was a man that was in line that I found very attractive. He ended up sitting alone, and so did I. Thinking back makes me feel like maybe I should've taken that initiative and sat with him, however when we were in the line, I did ask him a question, and he just sort of nodded his answer so hey I did my part to a certain extent. The major thing was I didn't do what I normally would've done, which is pounce, and put myself out there to make the first move. Throughout the rest of the lunch, I felt his eyes gravitate toward me. Mainly because mine gravitated towards him as well. As I sat at my table and debated about whether I was feeling, and seeing what I thought I was, or if it was all in my head. I wondered, what was holding him back from approaching me? I knew why I didn't approach him, but I'm sure I didn't have a "closed for business" sign on my forehead. It could be something personal the way it was with me or perhaps he too is on that seemingly long list of taken men. Either way, the opportunity, and chances were gone that day as soon as we left our separate tables without any exchange of communication. But at least I now know that I can patiently wait instead of jumping at every opportunity.

I've also had to make some changes when it comes to the things I watch, do, and even think. For instance, all those wedding shows that I enjoy watching. I like to see how they turn out, what the bride is wearing, but watching those shows have not helped with the original reason I started watching them, which was to get ideas for my wedding. I've concluded that I should stop watching them, so I've limited my TV watching. The reason why is that by watching those shows I usually end up dwelling on my situation, and the fact that I'm single. I start to think of my husband which we discussed before usually leads to other thoughts and actions. I haven't stopped watching them all together, but I have started to watch certain things in moderation. That goes for music as well. It's crazy to think of how music and all of the things that we take in daily, can have an influence on us. You just never know what hidden messages are in these things. Technology is a blessing and a curse. It's so easy to get caught in situations that lead to sin. Such as how easy it is to watch porn online. Sometimes you can't help what you stumble upon, but I'll admit that there were times when I'd purposely view some sites. Aside from getting turned on and sinning alongside the individuals on the screen I mostly end up feeling sorry for the people involved. Many of the videos online are of women doing any, and everything with men that don't care anything about them. Only God knows what possessed them to do these things on camera for the world. Thinking about the things I've seen are tempting even now, but nowadays I do my best to keep on my mind that no sin or habit is worth eternal damnation.

Aside from the everyday changes of the things I absorb, I'm also changing my mindset about certain things. I learned that some of the biggest changes must come from within, and that will ultimately change what your life looks like on the outside. These inner changes helped me realize that I needed to embrace myself, and my situation. How can I expect a man to love me when I wasn't fully showing love toward myself? I can't expect anyone to make me happy. That must come from within as well.

One woman told me "For Valentine's Day I buy a dozen roses and walk around in lingerie for myself!" "On the card, I write to myself, from myself!" It was funny to hear, and think about, but her words were inspiring to me. The main point of what she said is to love yourself. You can't depend on anyone else to make you happy, because happiness should come from within. I don't expect happiness to come from marriage, but I don't want marriage to be a dreadful thing. I've heard a lot of negative things about being married that sometimes make me question if that's how it is then what's the point?

Your grass can be green if you take the time to look at and tend to it! I've learned to stop looking over the fence at other people's grass and comparing. We must learn to be content with what we have. I know it's a struggle from time to time. The idea of being content is almost foreign to me because I'm personally always working toward other things, and moving forward, because I don't want to look back, and wonder where my life went. However, I'm grateful for the things I have even though I tend to focus on what I don't have more often.

I tagged along to window shop with a friend of mine. She had recently bought a new condo and was looking for furniture. At the end of the night, she gave me a tour of her place. The layout, appliances, levels, and size were great! Just when I started to compare where I'm living to her place in my mind, she showed me the water damage on one of the windows, and cabinets she had to replace. That scenario helped me put another into perspective. The same way I was comparing her place, and mine in my mind is the way a lot of us compare ourselves to others by looking at someone and wanting what they have. The overall package may look great, but we don't know about the water damage and other problems that come along with it, or the things that need to be fixed. The same can be said for relationships. I'm guilty of looking at my married friends, and wishing I was in their situation, and as I've mentioned before a few have told me at one time or another they've felt the same way about my life as a single woman. But just as I didn't know about the water damage in my friend's condo is the same way I don't know what's going on in my married friend's relationships. They could be having all types of problems, and here I am wishing I was them! You just never know what God is protecting you from. I heard someone say once that God will keep you even when you don't know you need to be kept.

Along with not comparing my situation to others, I'm also working on being comfortable with myself. I'm single, but I'm not impotent. There is no reason for me to sit around and wait until I'm married to enjoy certain things. I used to feel silly to think of doing things alone. I would find myself staying at home because I had no one to go anywhere with. Well, these days I've changed all of that because I have a new mind for a new time! Who says I can't eat at a sit-down restaurant alone? I've taken myself out to eat quite a few times now, and sat alone, and just enjoyed being out of the house. One day I decided to fulfill one of my fantasies. I've always dreamed of lying in the grass with my husband watching clouds go by, but I had never taken the time to just do it on my own. As I laid there and noticed all the beauty surrounding me, I felt at peace. It wasn't too hot or cold. The breeze and the clouds seemed to work together giving me an equal amount of sun, and shade. I concluded that I didn't need someone lying next to me to enjoy nature, and that beautiful day I would've missed if I was in my apartment. Being single doesn't mean you have to wait to go out, on the town, or that you can't take an evening to lie in the grass. Someone told me when I mentioned this idea that "a beautiful girl eating alone must look pitiful." But I say if you have the time, and the money to do it, then do it. If you want to lay in the grass and watch the clouds go by, do that too. Enjoy the time that you have. I find that time alone can be a special time for you, and God.

As much as I sometimes despise being single, I must admit that there are couples out there who are miserable too. That's why we can't associate gaining happiness with getting the things we want. It all must mean and be about more than your wants. Most of my friends are married or getting married, and I know that some of them aren't fond of it. There are even couples out there that barely even talk to each other. Communication is key in a relationship. Maybe this is just the opinion of a single woman, but I think that it shouldn't be hard to talk to your spouse. That's one reason that I want to make sure I marry the right person. I'm praying that we will be on the same page, and if we aren't that we can agree to disagree.

As the rain poured outside, I laid on my bed thinking that it was a great evening to be cuddled up with someone special, and maybe even a greater opportunity to do other things a married couple can do. I thought about one of my friends, and her husband, and hoped that they were taking advantage of what could be a romantic evening. I think I would try to take advantage of every moment I could have with my spouse. Part of me does not understand why some of my married friends, and I share the same problem when it comes to the lack of romance, and sex. Sex, romance, and communication should already be included in marriage in my book. I understand that your spouse must be in the mood for certain things, and that's because in my past I can remember not always being in the mood, but I believe that in my case my mood was not into it because I knew I wasn't married, and that there was no commitment behind the actions. It's hard to stay in the mood when you're thinking about how wrong it is. However, since the married couples don't have that restriction so I don't understand why we have the same issues. However, as I said before I have much to learn about being a wife.

"... Everybody wants to feel loved, but love will come. Don't settle for something like love when you can have the real thing. It will always end in disappointment

-Miracle Sims

CHAPTER - 11
LESSON LEARNED

| THE CULTIVATION PERIOD | LESSON LEARNED |

One of my friends told me that I'm going to be the perfect wife, because I'm getting all this knowledge, and advice about being in a relationship, and marriage beforehand. I must say that I am learning a lot. I feel that I've always been an understanding woman. But it seems to me that the women who are the least understanding are the ones in relationships. It makes me sometimes wonder what else is there about me besides the mindset I was in that is keeping me from being in a relationship. One evening when I was hanging out with my homegirl and her husband, I asked her husband why he thought I was single. His first response was "I don't know", but then he stated that it was "my choice". As much as I wanted to debate his opinion, I realized in a way he was right. I don't seem to have a problem attracting men, but now since I have a better outlook on life and the things, I want I've made it my mission not to settle for less than what, and who God has for me.

I've gotten a lot of advice, prayers, and encouragement since deciding to change my bad dating habits and focus on God's will. Some of the advice I've received are things I've already put in motion, such as waiting, and asking/telling God specifically what I want, and trusting that he will do it. I mentioned in the prologue about my long list that I wrote down of what I want in a man. This has brought some debate from one of my close friends, because she feels like my list-making is extreme, and that I'm looking for a perfectly packaged man. That's not exactly the case for me…I created the list not only to share with God what I wanted but to figure out for myself what I want. Before when I dated, I just focused on whether I was attracted to the individual or not then as I said before I would make him a prospect until proven not. Some things may seem extreme, but everything on my list was a quality that a man in my past may have had, and it is because of them I know a man can have these things; however, I think the extreme thing is having all the qualities in one person. But nothing is impossible with God, so I'm not worried about that. The other thing that concerns my friend about my list is she feels that I'm telling God what I want, even though He knows what I need. Sure, I'm telling him what I want, and I know He already knows what I need, but that is what prayer is all about. Right? In my opinion, I'm including God in this process. I'm willing to make exceptions to the list, and I know that he may not have all the qualities in the beginning, but that's the beauty of letting God be in control, because he already knows my needs, and wants. And since I now know my wants, it helps me to see clearly when the enemy tries to send someone my way that is not for me.

As I listened to one of my lady mentors pray for me, and my future husband I could do nothing, but smile, at how much her prayer coincided with my personal prayers. I've prayed for him a few times myself because he very well could be going through the same things I am. After my incident with Frank in Chapter 3 (The man who got me back on track), I realized that I wasn't ready for the type of man I want. Perhaps, if I had met "my one" before going through these changes, I would have probably pushed him away with my actions. Especially if he's already gone through the process that I'm going through now.

With every new day, there is a new lesson learned. Either by God giving me some enlightenment or through comments and advice from other people. As for my friend's comments about how amazed my husband will be about how good of a wife I will be. I can see that happening if I continue to put God first and apply the daily lessons, I've learned I know it will be worth it.

"I was such a fool

Searching life through, and through

For all the things that I

Already had in you....

I'm Alive, yeah!

Because your love has set me free!

I'm Alive, yeah!

Because your love made me believe, believe in me!"

Lyrics from: "Alive"
Written by: Miracle Sims, and Sha Chill

PART - III
FUTURE

CHAPTER - 12
CONFIRMATION, AND BLESSINGS

I have been attacked since I've decided to let God be the man in my life, but then again, I have had blessings, and benefits to come along with that decision as well. From confirmation of His words and promises to him laying on people's hearts to give me gifts, even a new car! As my family surprised me with my black 2007 Mustang, I couldn't help but think back on how I risked and compromised this blessing and the others I don't even know about by entertaining sin.

List of Advice, and Confirmations:
- **Do not dwell on the past,** *learn from the situation, and move forward.*
- **Wait.**
- **Focus on God**, *building a relationship with Him is the best, and the most important relationship we can ever have.*
- **Wait.**
- **Ask, and talk to God about what you want specifically, and trust that He will do it!**
- **Wait.**
- **Love yourself**, *you can't expect happiness to come from another person.*
- **Wait.**

- **Focus on the things you want to do.** *This is your time to focus on your goals and dreams.*
- **Wait.**
- **Be happy, and content with who you are, and what you have.** *There's only one of you!*
- **Wait.**
- **Don't be fooled by the devil's devices,** *for example, Men or Women that "seem" like the one, but aren't.*
- **Wait.**
- **Pray about every person you meet and become close with.** *If there's any doubt, let it go! There shouldn't be any doubt.*
- **Wait.**
- **When you get lonely, talk to God.** *He always wants to hear from you, and make sure you take the time to listen. Conversation works 2 ways, you know!*
- **Wait.**
- **Don't focus so much on "The One", but more on the right person God has for you.**
- **Wait.**
- **Wait for sex until marriage even after you meet the right one.** *Being physical taints the process of getting to know your mate.*
- **Wait!** PERIOD!

I'm sure you've noticed the constant repetition of the word "wait". Perhaps it was a little excessive, but it's necessary.

I've been working on my patience, and it is hard to do, but it will be worth it in the end.

It's hard trusting a God that you may not be able to see or hear physically, and it's bizarre to think you must trust Him with everything. EVERYTHING! But I've begun to stop trying to figure out what He's doing. There was one day that I broke down and had a big rant. I cried, yelled, and got out of so much tension to the point that I started to laugh, As I yelled "CAN'T YOU LET ME IN ON ANYTHING?!" I ended up realizing that the answer is no, not until, and unless he wants to. I must trust and believe that God would not have me go through all these changes and learn all these lessons in vain. In His timing, all will be revealed.

Again, we don't know what God could be protecting us from. We may be wanting something that isn't good for us. He is the only one who knows all. I want to encourage you to be thankful, content, and grateful for what you have. There are just some things in life we aren't meant to know. While we are trying to figure it out... God has already worked it out!

Cast not away, therefore, your confidence, which hath great recompense of reward. For ye have need of patience, that, after ye have done the will of God, ye might receive the promise.

Hebrews 10: 35-36
King James Version (KJV)

CHAPTER - 13
WORTH THE WAIT

Being single, and the way I was dealing with it led me into some bad habits. There have been many attempts to keep me from God, and the man He has for me. I see and understand that more now. My main problem was that I was basing relationships on being intimate. Intimacy is one part, but there is so much more involved in being in a relationship. I've had countless examples of being physical, and not getting to know much else about the man past how he could make me feel, sexually. I realized this when I tried to envision my husband without thinking of anything sexual. My thoughts didn't get very far before they ended up physical, so I stopped trying. It showed me that I do want a man for the wrong reasons.

Everything I've learned daily is a blessing. This cultivation period that I'm going through has helped me truly realize what is important. Marriage is a covenant God respects. He doesn't want us to be alone. That's why he made Eve for Adam. However, even though it's great to want marriage, and a family, those things aren't our purpose. We were created to love God and show His love to others. Once you are married your spouse becomes your "one", and I want to trust God's knowledge and plan when it comes to that. Having a husband or wife is a serious thing. It is now your job to show your spouse how much God loves them. We know that God is a jealous God and if He gave me my husband right now, or before I gained this knowledge, I probably would've placed all my attention on him and lost sight of what is truly important. My relationship with God. It's so easy to forget that the correct way to love is God, others, and then yourself. Imagine if we all put God first and loved others as we love ourselves. If we lived that way, I believe that there would be world peace. More than half of the sins we commit every day would be extinct with just loving God because if we loved Him and put Him first, we wouldn't commit any sins because we know that it wouldn't please Him.

Sometimes I tend to debate if my sacrifices and change of heart will be in vain. I wonder if my husband is going through half of what I'm going through while I wait for him. I also wonder if there is a man out there that wants the things I want. However, I am working on changing all of these thoughts, because they are all just negative thinking. I must keep faith and believe that God will keep His promises in all things.

Some situations are easier than others to deny. Since my decision, I've had to deny not only myself but handsome men, even married ones who've made physical advances. But I know what I want, and that does not include more random hookups, or borrowing someone else's man. I want my own. Never mind how attractive they may be, I can't waste my time thinking about a married man! I feel stronger when I do not give in to the temptations that come my way, and it is quite liberating not having to worry month to month about the possibility of being pregnant. I had so much nervousness and stress in my life before, and it feels great to know that I'm free, and no matter what comes against me, God has it all under control. Despite the day-to-day struggle, I know that in the end, my struggle will not be in vain. I've come too far to go back to the way I used to be.

There is no black, and white, step-by-step guide to being single. My prayer is that you take my story and do what I didn't do. Learn, and apply what is meant for you in your life, so you don't make the mistakes that I did. I think we take for granted the parents that tell us that very same sentiment. But they are right, there are some things we don't have to go through. There were things that I did that I knew were wrong, and I have suffered the consequences of my choices. Because of my choices, I now must go back and reach to be the woman I should've been the whole time. I know I'm not perfect, and I don't expect my husband to be, however when it comes to being single, I've chosen to set my mind on God, and wait for Him to send me the best, and nothing less. Not someone that might fit, or may work out. The best, because that's what He wants for all of us. Perhaps I'll fill you in on how married life is when that time comes. But until then,

Peace, and Much Love,
"Miracle"

EPILOGUE

Hello Friends!

Thank you for reading "The Cultivation Period". I pray it was useful and informative. The majority of this book was written in my 20's under a different title, and for an entirely different reason. However, so much has happened since then. Some good, some bad, some great, and wonderful! Now at the age of 35, I'm happy to report that the majority of the things I was thinking and praying about then I am now living, and have now! I am the wife of an amazing and supportive gentleman, name Nadario Seays and the mother of our annoyingly adorable son, Nadario Jr aka NJ and I wouldn't trade this life for the world! I would say that the choices I made during my cultivation period were not in vain, and although I can't say that I did everything "right" I can see how God allowed all things to work together for my good! I often think back on the different crossroads that I came across in my life, and I wonder where I would've been if I had chosen a different path? What would I be doing? Do I have any regrets? No, not really... I believe that each issue, choice, and decision helped me not only to be who I am, but these experiences have furthermore helped me to appreciate where I am all the more! Again, I hope and pray that hearing the details of my life and testimony will encourage and inspire you to trust God and his marvelous plan for your life. Choices are truly life-changing my friends, and in my humble opinion, it would behoove us all to stop trying to write our own stories... hand over the pen, and trust the true Author, our Lord and Savior Jesus Christ!"

SPECIAL THANKS

First giving honor to God. He is truly the author of this book. It is amazing how well everything came together for me. This started as an idea, and a notebook, and from there the words practically plastered themselves on the pages. It's amazing looking at the work He's done with this project, and the work He's done in my life. I'm so thankful that He is a God of a second, third, fourth, and even fifth chance. I pray that those of you who read this will open your mind to the ideas, and things He's saying to you through me. If things are sticking out and are sounding like your life it is Him, not me. I'm not that smart to know what's going on in every single woman, or person's life. Like I said in the book I can only speak of my experiences.

I give honor to my family. Mother Evangelist Evelyn O'Neal, if not for your teaching about our heavenly Father I have no idea where I would be. Yes, I do, I would be nowhere...I'd be lost. To my Father, Larry O'Neal, Dad I appreciate you being there and allowing God to use you to bless me in so many ways from helping to keep a roof over my head to many other ways I don't even know. To my sister, Nila O'Neal for your ongoing love, and support. Keep on keeping on my sister! To my friend M.D Bryant and her husband Kareem, I pray that God continues to bless both of you and bless your marriage. I appreciate the many conversations, and times we've had just hanging out. You guys have never once made me feel like a third wheel. You don't know how great that is. To the countless family and friends such as my mentor Mrs. Dee Janes, and my brother from another mother Kelvin Carter, and various others, who allowed God to minister to me through their advice. You've blessed me so much you don't even know. My heart is full! To the readers again thank you for taking out the time to read this. I pray that you are as blessed reading as I was blessed writing.

To my guys in Pakistan, Arsal and Sami! Thank you so much from the bottom of my heart! Both of you gentlemen have been such a blessing in my life, your patience, and kindness throughout the creation of this and all of the projects that we've collaborated on since 2020 has not gone unnoticed and is truly appreciated!

ABOUT THE AUTHOR

Wife and Mother of One, Miracle Sims is a versatile talent! Since she received her Associate's Degree in theatre at Gordon College in 2006, she has been acting, writing, singing, and songwriting independently. She is currently the owner of several business endeavors; Miracle Plays, Unwine: Self-Care and Sips Spa. She is also host and creator of the podcast and talk show "God, Sex, and Love" and author of The Juice: 30-Day Bible Study Journal, The Wine Amateur: Wine Tasting Journal, and Unwine: Selfcare Coloring Book for Women!

Visit GodSexandLove.com to watch her weekly talk show and/or listen to her podcast for daily inspiration!

linktr.ee/actressmiraclesims

Made in the USA
Columbia, SC
13 December 2024